HEY PURPLE HAND GANG!

Are you ready to test your super sp...
amazing search-and-find adventur...
some of them are really h...

Good luck!

Henry

What's lost?

Henry's fiendish friends and evil enemies have each lost one of their favourite possessions – they're listed throughout the book, see if you can spot them!

But wait, there's even more to look for! Can you spy Henry's awesome best presents ever?

Mega Whirl Goo Shooter

Super Soaker 2000

Whoopee Cushion

The Smellie Bellies' Greatest Hits CD

Mega-gigantic TV

Bugle Blast Boots

Dungeon Drink Kit

Roller Bowlers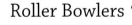

How about Perfect Peter's stupid boring awful nappy baby wish list?

Initialed handkerchief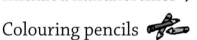

Colouring pencils

Books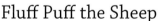

Daffy and her Dancing Daisies Greatest Hits CD

Fluff Puff the Sheep

Don't forget ME, I'm hiding somewhere on every page!

And keep your eyes peeled for fiendish fowl, Dolores the Chicken!

Horrid Henry's Birthday Bash

How many of the following can you find?

Presents

Slices of cake

Balloons

Jellies

'What's lost?' item:

Miss Battle-Axe's whistle

Wish list item:

Horrid Henry's whoopee cushion

Don't forget to look out for Dolores!

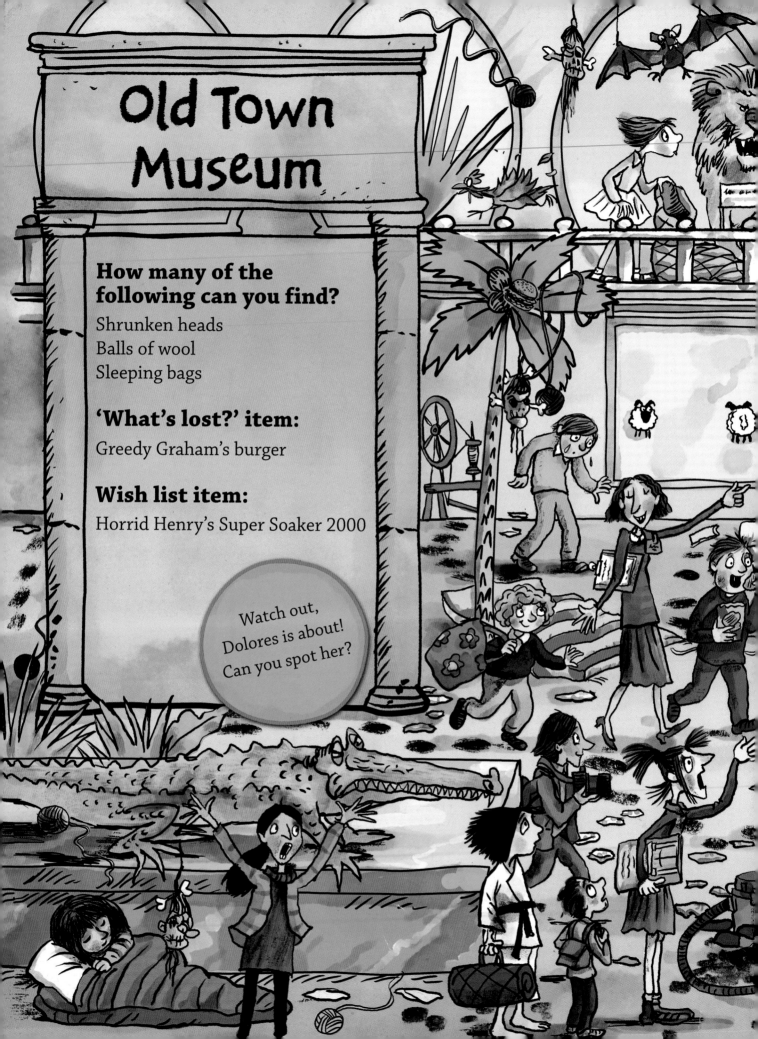

Christmas Chaos

How many of the following can you find?

Stockings
Christmas crackers
Scarves

'What's lost?' item:

Rude Ralph's Purple Hand Gang flag

Wish list item:

Horrid Henry's Roller Bowlers

Hopefully Dad doesn't mistake Dolores the chicken for a turkey! Find her, quick!

Scruff's Pet Show

How many of the following can you find?
Rosettes
Bones
Leads

'What's lost?' item:
Perfect Peter's cello

Wishlist items:
Perfect Peter's *Daffy and her Dancing Daisies Greatest Hits* CD
Horrid Henry's Mega Whirl Goo Shooter

With so many animals running wild, keeping an eye out for deadly Dolores is going to be tricky …

SCRUFF'S PET SHOW

School Sports Day

How many of the following can you find?

Eggs and spoons
Flags
Medals

'What's lost?' item:

Horrid Henry's teddy, Mr Kill

Wishlist item:

Perfect Peter's pile of boring school books

Dolores the chicken loves an egg and spoon race. Find her before she steals all of the eggs!

Camp Cramp

How many of the following can you find?
Toilet rolls
Bugs
Sausages

'What's lost?' item:
Singing Soraya's microphone

Wishlist item:
Horrid Henry's *Smellie Bellies' Greatest Hits* CD

Quick, hide! Henry's spotted Miss Battle-Axe by the loos – can you find his sneaky spying spot?

Horrid Henry's Haunted House

How many of the following can you find?
Spiders
Skulls
Bats

'What's lost?' item:
Perfect Peter's handkerchief

Wishlist item:
Horrid Henry's Dungeon
Drink Kit

Zombies, ghosts, Moody Margaret – aargh, the terror! Plus, fiendish fowl Dolores is still on the loose, beware!

Answers

Here's
Horrid Henry!

Horrid Henry's Birthday Bash

How many of the following can you find?
Presents
Slices of cake
Balloons
Jellies

'What's lost?' item:
Miss Battle-Axe's whistle

Wish list item:
Horrid Henry's whoopee cushion

Don't forget to look out for Dolores!

There are:
11 presents, 7 slices of cake,
11 balloons, 4 jellies

Miss Battle-Axe's whistle
is on the floor next to
Greedy Graham

Henry's whoopee cushion is
on the sofa

Here's
Horrid Henry!

There are:
10 raffle tickets, 5 bags of
crisps, 3 lunchboxes

Moody Margaret's trumpet
is on top of the bunting

Henry's mega-gigantic TV
is under the cake stall

School Summer Fete

How many of the following can you find?
Raffle tickets
Bags of crisps
Lunchboxes

'What's lost?' item:
Moody Margaret's trumpet

Wish list item:
Horrid Henry's mega-gigantic TV

Look out for Dolores the chicken – she's on the loose!

FROSTY FREEZE ICE CREAM

Here's
Horrid Henry!

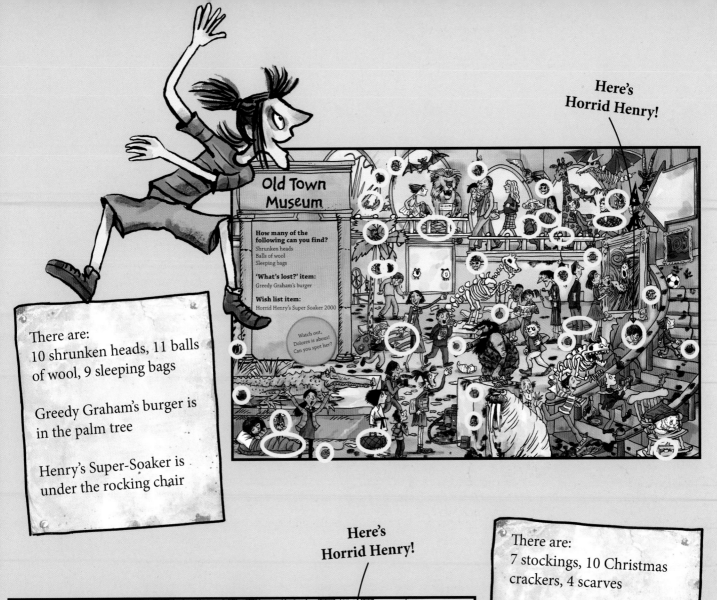

There are:
10 shrunken heads, 11 balls
of wool, 9 sleeping bags

Greedy Graham's burger is
in the palm tree

Henry's Super-Soaker is
under the rocking chair

Old Town Museum

How many of the
following can you find?
Shrunken heads
Balls of wool
Sleeping bags

'What's lost?' item:
Greedy Graham's burger

Wish list item:
Horrid Henry's Super Soaker 2000

Watch out,
Dolores is about!
Can you spot her?

Here's
Horrid Henry!

Christmas Chaos

How many of the
following can you find?
Stockings
Christmas crackers
Scarves

'What's lost?' item:
Rude Ralph's Purple Hand Gang flag

Wish list item:
Horrid Henry's Roller
Bowlers

Hopefully Dad
doesn't mistake
Dolores the chicken
for a turkey!
Find her, quick!

There are:
7 stockings, 10 Christmas
crackers, 4 scarves

Rude Ralph's Purple
Hand Gang flag is on the
Christmas tree

Henry's Roller Bowlers
are next to Moody
Margaret

SPECIAL

There are:
10 buckets, 12 shells,
9 crabs, 9 ice creams

Aerobic Al's trainers are
near Lazy Linda

Perfect Peter's colouring
pencils are under
Granny's foot

Here's
Horrid Henry!

Sandy Bottom Beach

How many of the following can you find?
Buckets
Shells
Crabs
Ice creams

'What's lost?' item:
Aerobic Al's trainers

Wishlist item:
Perfect Peter's colouring pencils

Blecccccch, Henry hates the beach. Luckily he's found the perfect spot to spend the day...

Here's
Horrid Henry!

Scruff's Pet Show

SCRUFF'S PET SHOW

How many of the following can you find?
Rosettes
Bones
Leads

'What's lost?' item:
Perfect Peter's cello

Wishlist items:
Perfect Peter's *Daffy and her Dancing Daisies Greatest Hits* CD
Horrid Henry's Mega Whirl Goo Shooter

With so many animals running wild, keeping an eye out for deadly Dolores is going to be tricky.

There are: 5 rosettes, 12 bones, 5 leads

Perfect Peter's cello is on top of the red tunnel

Perfect Peter's *Daffy and her Dancing Daisies Greatest Hits* CD is next to Dolores the chicken

Henry's Mega Whirl Goo Shooter is under the 'Scruff's Pet Show' banner

Here's
Horrid Henry!

Mellow Mall

How many of the following can you find?
Pigeons
Shopping baskets
Chips

'What's lost?' items:
Bossy Bill's photocopy
of his bum

Wishlist items:
Horrid Henry's Bugle Blast Boots
Perfect Peter's Fluff Puff the Sheep

Henry's hiding from Mum – she's going to make him try on school trousers! Can you find him first?

There are:
11 pigeons, 8 shopping baskets, 15 chips

Bossy Bill's photocopy of his bum is under the sandwich board

Henry's Bugle Blast Boots are beside the food tent

Perfect Peter's Fluff Puff the Sheep is outside the shoe shop

Here's
Horrid Henry!

There are: 6 eggs and spoons, 11 flags, 5 medals

Henry's teddy, Mr Kill, is next to the red flag at the top of the racetrack

Perfect Peter's pile of school books is next to Greedy Graham

School Sports Day

How many of the following can you find?
Egg and spoons
Flags
Medals

'What's lost?' item:
Horrid Henry's teddy
Mr Kill

Wishlist item:
Perfect Peter's pile of boring school books

Dolores the chicken loves an egg and spoon race. Find her before she steals all of the eggs!

Here's
Horrid Henry!

Camp Cramp

How many of the following can you find?
Toilet rolls
Bugs
Sausages

'What's lost?' item:
Singing Soraya's microphone

Wishlist item:
Horrid Henry's *Smellie Bellies'* Greatest Hits CD

Quick, hide! Henry's spotted Miss Battle-Axe by the loos – can you find his sneaky spying spot?

There are:
10 toilet rolls, 10 bugs,
10 sausages

Singing Soraya's microphone
is in Jolly Josh's tent

Henry's *Smellie Bellie's Greatest Hits* CD is in the
back window of the car

Horrid Henry's Haunted House

How many of the following can you find?
Spiders
Skulls
Bats

'What's lost?' item:
Perfect Peter's hankerchief

Wishlist item:
Horrid Henry's Dungeon Drink

Zombies, ghosts, Moody Margaret – aargh, the terror! Plus, fiendish fowl Dolores is still on the loose, beware!

There are:
15 spiders, 8 skulls, 9 bats

Perfect Peter's handkerchief is
behind Dad

Henry's Dungeon Drink Kit
is next to Mum

Here's
Horrid Henry!